Hear Me Out

2

David Nunan
Noriko Tomioka

NATIONAL
GEOGRAPHIC
L E A R N I N G

JN116673

Australia · Brazil · Mexico · Singapore · United Kingdom · United States

Hear Me Out 2 [Text Only]

Originally written by David Nunan and adapted by Noriko Tomioka

Photo Credits:
p. 16: © Siri Stafford/DigitalVision/Thinkstock; p. 17: (t to b) © dolgachov/iStock/Thinkstock, © moodboard/moodboard/Thinkstock, © lila-esiStock/Thinkstock; p. 18: (l to r, t to b) © m-imagephotography/iStock/Thinkstock, © g-stockstudio/iStock/Thinkstock, © monkeybusinessimages/iStock/Thinkstock, © IPGGutenbergUKLtd/iStock/Thinkstock; p. 28: (t to b) © amanaimagesRF/Thinkstock, © Poike/iStock/Thinkstock; p. 30: (l to r) © Ron Chapple Stock/Ron Chapple Studios/Thinkstock, © Ingram Publishing/Thinkstock, © Jacob Wackerhausen/ iStock/Thinkstock, © Purestock/Thinkstock; p. 36: (t to b, l to r) © Top Photo Corporation/Top Photo Group/Thinstock, © JanelleLugge/iStock/Thinkstock, © Hans-Peter Merten/Getty Images, © wrangel/iStock/Thinkstock, © Shanenk/iStock/Thinkstock, © LiveLifeTraveling/iStock/ Thinkstock; p. 41: (l to r) © Dave J Hogan/Getty Images Entertainment/Getty Images, © Kevin Mazur/Getty Images Entertainment/Getty Images, © Martin Mills/Archive Photos/Getty Images; p. 52: (t to b) © Creatas Images/Creatas/Thinkstock, © yacobchuk/iStock/Thinkstock, © Ridofranz/ iStock/Thinkstock, © milan2099/iStock/Thinkstock; p. 63: (l to r) © Kevin Forest/Photodisc/ Thinkstock, © Carlos Restrepo/iStock/Thinkstock, © Jupiterimages/PHOTOS.com»/Thinkstock, © mizoula/iStock/Thinkstock; p. 75: © shironosov/iStock/Thinkstock; p. 79: (t to b) © Steve Mason/ DigitalVision/Thinkstock, © Jupiterimages/Pixland/Thinkstock; p. 88: (l to r) © Ridofranz/iStock/ Thinkstock, © Jupiterimages/liquidlibrary/Thinkstock, © RonOrmanJr/iStock/Thinkstock, © XiXinXing/iStock/Thinkstock; p. 90: (l to r) © Comstock/Stockbyte/Thinkstock, © XiXinXing/ iStock/Thinkstock, © XiXinXing/iStock/Thinkstock, © Chris Knorr / Design Pics/Valueline/ Thinkstock; p. 95: © Jacob Wackerhausen/iStock/Thinkstock

For permission to use material from this textbook or product, e-mail to **eltjapan@cengage.com**

ISBN: 978-4-86312-321-2

Cengage Learning K.K.
No. 2 Funato Building 5th Floor
1-11-11 Kudankita, Chiyoda-ku
Tokyo 102-0073
Japan

Tel: 03-3511-4392
Fax: 03-3511-4391

はしがき

　2010年に『Step-by-Step Listening』が刊行されてから、早くも6年が経ちます。このテキストの改訂を考え始めたとき、まさしくその依頼をセンゲージ ラーニングよりいただき、この『Hear Me Out 2』の編著を手がけることになりました。『Hear Me Out』というタイトルの新シリーズで、そのレベル2（中級）として、『Step-by-Step Listening』を改訂したものが本書です。

　この改訂版発刊の流れを元へたどれば、同じくセンゲージ ラーニングの『Listen In, Book 2』（David Nunan 著）がこれらの原著となります。以前、この『Listen In, Book 2』を気に入って長く使用していましたが、日本の学生向けにアレンジしたいと思い始めた折、センゲージ ラーニングから和書化への協力の依頼をタイミングよくいただき、『Step-by-Step Listening』の編著を手がけたのです。さらにこのテキストをパワーアップさせるため、今回の改訂では平易な問題を削減したり、難易度を上げた問題に変更したりするとともに、原著『Listen In, Book 2』から各ユニットに即した問題の追加も行いました。その結果、リスニングのテキストとして充実したボリュームのある内容にしたいという思いを本書『Hear Me Out 2』で実現できました。CD2枚分の音声を提供することで、学生による予習そして復習においても聞き応えのある教材となっています。

　各ユニットは6ページとなり、じっくりと各設問に取り組めるように問題を構成しました。音声はすべて『Listen In, Book 2』のものを再使用しています。この音声にこだわるのは、自然な英語の速さを体感できるからです。この原著の持ち味を活かしつつ、日本の学生がスピード感のある英語でリスニング学習を重ねることにより、自然な英語に馴染めるように問題構成に配慮しました。

　各ユニットの導入部は、そのユニットで使用される語彙についての予備演習としています。段階的に平易な問題から難易度を高めながら、多角的に問題を作ったことで、内容理解がよくできるような展開となっています。問題内容に少しくどさを感じるところがあるかもしれません。しかし、何度も音声を耳に馴染ませることにより、最後には音声にしたがってシャドーイングすることができるようになっていただきたいので、聴解力を高めるための繰り返しのトレーニングと理解して学習に臨んでください。

　また、イラストや写真などが減ったため、『Step-by-Step Listening』よりもビジュアル的にはシンプルな紙面の仕上がりとなりました。豊富な音声量とそれに付随する問題量によって、集中してリスニングに取り組める工夫がなされています。

　TOEICやTOEFLなどの資格試験に重点が置かれる現在、学生の皆さんがこれらの試験のリスニング問題対策にいきなり取り組むのは難しいでしょう。リスニングが苦手な場合、まずは本書で聴解力を鍛えてから、資格試験のリスニング問題対策に取り組むと良い効果が得られます。この『Hear Me Out 2』が皆さんの英語の聴解力を伸ばす助けになるものと信じます。

　最後に、内容の構成やレイアウトなどにおいて、いろいろな助言をいただき、サポートしてくださったセンゲージ ラーニング株式会社と有限会社パラスタイルの編集担当の方々に心からの謝意を表します。

編著者

音声ファイルの利用方法

ヘッドホン・アイコンがある箇所の音声は、すべてオンラインで再生またはダウンロードすることができます。

https://ngljapan.com/hmo2-audio/

❶ 上記のURLにアクセス、またはQRコードをスマートフォンなどのリーダーでスキャン
❷ 表示されるファイル名をクリックして音声ファイルを再生またはダウンロード

Contents

本書は英語の聴解力向上を目指す教材です。テーマ別に分かれた15ユニットから成り、日常的なトピックに沿ったリスニングが中心となっています。1つのユニットは6ページ構成です。各ユニットには6つまたは7つの演習問題（Task）があり、その後のYour Turn! では、ユニットの学習テーマに沿った内容の会話練習へと発展できるようになっています。そして、最後のIn Focusでは、少しスピードの速い英語の聴き取り問題に挑戦します。

以下では、ユニット内の演習問題やアクティビティの特徴を具体的に述べるとともに、本書の効果的な使用方法を説明します。

1

ユニットに出てくる語彙に関する問題です。わからない語彙は辞書で意味を調べ、その語彙が使われている文脈に注意しながら解答を探りましょう。

2 〜 7

音声を繰り返し聴き、問題の解答を探っていきます。簡単な導入問題である A から、選択肢問題、内容真偽問題、記述式問題の B や C へと発展していきます。問題をヒントに音声を何回も聴くことで、聴き取った内容の理解を深めていきましょう。じっくりと取り組み、確信が持てる解答が得られるまで、何回も繰り返し聴いてください。

Listen for it

注意すべき表現が簡単かつ的確に説明されているので、参考にしてみましょう。

演習問題に取り組むポイント

1 わからない単語は労力を惜しまず、辞書で意味を調べることが大切です。面倒かもしれませんが、この作業は少しでも意味が頭に残る助けとなります。

2 これは使える表現だと思ったら、何度も声に出して言ってみたり、何度も書いたりして、自分のものにしていきましょう。このように繰り返し練習することで、英語の表現が豊かになっていきます。

3 質問に答える記述式の問題では、英文で解答することに徹します。ただし、文で解答することが難しい場合は、語句で解答しても構いませんが、単語1つだけで解答しないように心がけましょう。

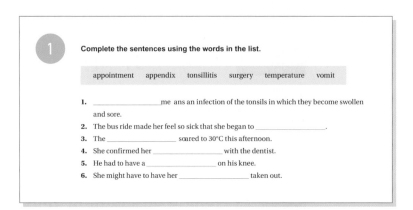

1 Complete the sentences using the words in the list.

| appointment | appendix | tonsillitis | surgery | temperature | vomit |

1. _____ me ans an infection of the tonsils in which they become swollen and sore.
2. The bus ride made her feel so sick that she began to _____.
3. The _____ soared to 30°C this afternoon.
4. She confirmed her _____ with the dentist.
5. He had to have a _____ on his knee.
6. She might have to have her _____ taken out.

5

A Listen to the radio broadcast. Number the topics in the order the doctor talks about them (1–4).

- Exercise ____
- Diet ____
- Smoking ____
- Sleep ____

Listen for it

Overdo means to do too much of something, such as dieting or exercising.

B Listen again and write down Dr. Bain's tips on maintaining good health.

Dr. Bain's E-Z Tips for Healthy Living

Exercise
....
Diet
....
Smoking
....
Sleep

C Listen again and circle *T* for *True* or *F* for *False*.

1. To eat a nutritious diet, you have to give up the foods you love. **T / F**
2. Artificially produced vitamins cannot be a substitute for the nutrition we derive from food. **T / F**
3. You need at least eight hours of sleep a night. **T / F**
4. To maintain good fitness, thirty minutes' exercise is enough. **T / F**
5. You must not overdo vitamins or alcohol. **T / F**

Your Turn!

Asking and talking about special events

Try this . . .

Think of a family or friend event you attended. Make a conversation about it.

- Have you been to a family or friend event recently?
  — Yes, I have been to my _____.
- What was it like?
  — Well, the wedding/reception/food was _____.
- How many people turned up?
  — I guess around _____.
- So, was it fun?

In Focus   Crying in the chapel

Listen and fill in the following blanks to complete the passage.   ◉ T-04

Is marriage obsolete? Since the 1950s, _____ numbers of married couples and _____ divorce rates have led some to believe that it is. But huge numbers of people continue to _____ marriage as an important life goal, and the vast majority will marry at least _____ in their lifetime. One reason people regard marriage so highly is that it can _____ people with a source of emotional _____, mutual _____, and lasting _____.

Your Turn!

いよいよ皆さんが主役になる番です。スピーキングに馴れていなくても、安心してください。会話の導入となる例文をいくつか挙げているので、最初はこれらをヒントとして利用したり、同じユニット内の演習問題で聴いた会話を参考にしたりして、会話練習をやってみましょう。

In Focus

ユニットのテーマに関連した文章のナレーションを聴きながら、空欄になっている単語をキャッチして記入し、英文を完成させる問題です。ただし、このセクションの音声は教師用 CD だけに収録されています（p.4 に記載のウェブサイトでは提供されていません）。少し速いスピードで読まれているので、予習時に英文に目を通し、わからない語句等は辞書で調べて、おおよその内容を推測した上で、授業での聴き取り練習に臨みましょう。

●日本語に取り巻かれた環境のなか、英語のリスニング能力を高めることは容易ではありません。初めはまったく聴き取れず、落胆することもあるかと思いますが、聴解力の向上は英語の音声に接する時間数に比例します。さらに効果的に学習を行うには、ただ聞き流すのではなく、演習問題を解きながら、根気よく耳に馴染ませる努力が必要です。音声をよく聴き、あとについてリピートできるくらいまで練習を重ねてください。たとえば、音声ファイルをダウンロードして通学時間を利用して聴いたり、部屋で音楽を聞いて過ごす時間を本書の音声を聴く時間に変えたりするのもよいでしょう。とにかく英語を耳に馴らすことが大切です。初めはなかなか聴き取れませんが、根気よく続けていくと、このテキストでの学習を終える頃には、自分の聴解力の変化にきっと気付くはずです。

Asking and answering personal information questions

1   **Complete the sentences using the words in the list.**

boarding call	carousel	duty-free
boarding pass	immigration	baggage claim area

1.   She lifted her luggage off the _____.

2.   At the check-in counter, you receive your _____.

3.   This is the final _____ for Air Pacific flight 451 to Hong Kong.

4.   We landed at Heathrow and went through customs and _____.

5.   Collect your luggage at the _____.

6.   She bought 400 cigarettes at the airport _____ shop.

2   **Listen and complete the following scripts.**

CD1
02
▼
05

1.   Dr. Alice Turner, please come to the All-Asia Airways _____ immediately.

2.   Can you tell Professor Carter there's a _____ on line one in the airport office?

3.   This is the final boarding call for flight _____ to Hong Kong. Would Ms. Theresa Vanderpyl and Mr. Oliver Tam please come immediately to _____?

4.   Would incoming passengers on flight _____ please proceed to carousel number _____ to pick up your luggage?

3

Singapore Immigration Service   Arrival Card

Arrival Card Number   **Welcome to Singapore**

000 0000 00 000

Family Name

First (Given) Name(s)

Sex   Passport Number

☐ Male   ☐ Female

Flight No./Vessel Name/Vehicle No.

Last City/Port of Embarkation

Address in Singapore

Length of Stay

☐☐☐ Days   _____

                              Signature

B **Listen again and circle *T* for *True* or *F* for *False*.**

1. The woman needs some help to fill in the arrival card.   **T / F**
2. The man has come from Singapore.   **T / F**
3. She can sign the card without her glasses.   **T / F**

4

Imagine you are at Immigration in the United States. Listen and circle the best response.

1. a. Sure. There you go.
    b. No, I'm sorry.
    c. Yes, I had one issued recently.

2. a. Yes, I've been here before.
    b. No, I haven't.
    c. No, this is my second time.

3. a. In the United States.
    b. For five days.
    c. At the Downtown Hotel.

4. a. In the United States.
    b. For five days.
    c. At the Downtown Hotel.

5. a. Yes, I do. Here it is.
    b. On the 16th.
    c. Here's my passport.

6. a. My next stop is Montreal.
    b. I'm not sure.
    c. I'm attending a conference.

5

A   Oliver is answering questions about the services at an airport. Listen to Part 1 of the conversation and answer the following questions.

Listen for it

You're telling me, with stress on *me*, is used to agree strongly with something another person says.

1. What is Oliver doing now?

    _____

2. What is Oliver's last name?

    _____

3. Which title does he prefer, Mr. or Dr.?

    _____

4. Where did he come from?

    _____

5. What is his nationality?

    _____

B Listen to Part 2 of the conversation and note his comments.

About the airport	
Arrival area	
Immigration	
Duty free	
General appearance	

6

A Listen and circle the best answer.

1. This is . . .
   a. a survey.
   b. an interview.
   c. a face-to-face conversation.

2. The people who are talking . . .
   a. are coworkers.
   b. are friends.
   c. do not know each other.

3. They are . . .
   a. in an office.
   b. at an airport.
   c. at a hotel.

4. According to the woman, the bags were . . .
   a. lost.
   b. stolen.
   c. delayed.

B **Listen again and complete the information on the form.**

CD1
15

Missing Baggage Details			
Flight number:		From:	
Passenger Name: Mr./Ms.			
Number of Bags:		Phone:	
Local Address:			

7 **Listen and complete the following scripts.**

CD1
16
18

1. Panair Airways regrets to announce the _____ of its flight from
    _____. The flight is now expected to arrive at _____.
    Panair Airways regrets any inconvenience caused.

2. **M:** Hey Gladys, your Uncle Bob is late, so we'll be there about _____.
    What does he look like again?
    W: Well, he's _____ height, heavyset. Aunt Muriel says fat, but he
    thinks it's _____. Ha-ha-ha. Anyway, he has a beard.
    M: OK, he should be easy enough to find.

3. **M1:** Hello, Bob?
    M2: Hi. You must be Jim. Pleased to meet you. Sorry about the delayed flight.
    M1: Oh, that's OK. Not your _____. Here, the car's parked over here.
    Let me help you with your _____.

Your Turn!

Asking and answering personal information questions

Try this . . .

Imagine you are an airline passenger. You've lost your glasses and can't read the arrival card. Ask your partner to fill it in for you.

- What's your name?
- Can you tell me your nationality?
- Where did you come from?
- Where do you live?
- Where are you planning to stay in the United States?

| Immigration Service U.S.A. | **Arrival Card** |

Welcome to the United States Admission Number

000 , 0000 , 00 , 000

Family Name

First (Given) Name   Birth Date (Day/Month/Year)

Sex   Country of Citizenship

Male   Female

Passport Number   Airline and Flight Number

Country Where You Live

City Where You Boarded

Address While in the United States

Signature

In Focus ## The future of travel

Listen and fill in the following blanks to complete the passage.   T-02

To some people, taking a "dream [1]_____" might mean suntanning on the beach in Bali, trekking through the Himalayas, or [2]_____ in the Swiss Alps. But how about spending a relaxing week at the bottom of the [3]_____ or blasting off for a fun-filled trip into [4]_____ space? Sound impossible? Many experts [5]_____ that vacations like these could be widely [6]_____ within as little as [7]_____ years—albeit at a very high [8]_____.

Unit

2 Describing people

1 **Complete the sentences using the words in the list.**

> dating agency   intelligent   beard   outgoing   bald   mustache

1. He is friendly and _____.
2. He met his wife through a _____.
3. Chimpanzees are _____ enough to use sign language.
4. His features were disguised by dark glasses and a false _____.
5. His upper lip was covered with a small _____.
6. He combs his hair forward to cover his _____ spot.

2 **A** **Listen. How do the women describe the men? Circle the words you hear in each conversation.**

1. interesting / intelligent / creative / shy / gentle
2. smart / kind / funny / nice / boring
3. interesting / intelligent / handsome / talkative / strange

B **Listen again and fill in the following blanks.**

1. a. They arranged to meet at _____ o'clock.
   b. The woman said Michael is _____ and _____.

2. Felix has a _____.

3. a. What does Derek do?   He is _____.
   b. The dating agency is waiting for _____.

3

A Megan is talking to someone from a dating agency. Listen and complete the form.

CD1 22

Listen for it

Mm-hmm is used to express agreement, understanding, or to express an affirmative answer.

PerfectMatch Inc.

Name: *Megan Johnson*

Interests:

- ☑ Books   Kinds: *biographies*
- ☐ Music   Kinds: _____
- ☐ Movies   Kinds: _____
- ☐ Sports   Kinds: _____

Person looking for:

- Shares same interests?   ☐ Yes   ☐ No   ☐ Doesn't matter
- Personal qualities: _____
- Appearance: ☐ Important   ☐ Not important

B Listen again and answer the following questions.

CD1 22

1. What kind of person is she looking for?

   _____

2. What is important to her?

   It is what is _____.

3. Why is it easy for the dating agency to find a man for her?

   _____

A **Listen and circle *T* for *True* or *F* for *False*.**

1. Geoff is an energetic person.   **T / F**
2. Tony is outgoing.   **T / F**
3. Mick describes himself as quiet.   **T / F**

B **Listen again and write what each person likes and doesn't like.**

	Name	Likes	Doesn't like
1.	Geoff		
2.	Tony		
3.	Mick		

A **Listen and circle *T* for *True* or *F* for *False*.**

1. She likes people who are kind.   **T / F**
2. She is looking for someone who is handsome.   **T / F**
3. She is energetic.   **T / F**
4. She likes sports.   **T / F**
5. She likes the theater.   **T / F**
6. She likes reading.   **T / F**

B Listen again and complete the form with Claudia's information.

Best Matchmaker

Name: _Claudia Wilson_

Interests:

☐ Books   Kinds: _____

☐ Music   Kinds: _____

☐ Movies Kinds: _____

☐ Sports Kinds: _____

Person looking for:

• Shares same interests?   ☐ Yes   ☐ No   ☐ Doesn't matter

• Personal qualities: _____

• Appearance: ☐ Important   ☐ Not important

6

A Listen to the conversation and match the personality traits to the correct people. Some words are used more than once.

Nancy

John

- hardworking -
- reliable -
- honest -
- curious -
- independent -
- friendly -
- efficient -
- dedicated -

Paul

Gina

B **Listen again and describe the negative points for the following people.**

CD1
27

- **John** _____
- **Nancy** _____
- **Gina** _____

Your Turn!

Describing people

Try this . . .

You are talking to someone from a dating agency. Ask your partner the questions and complete the form with his/her information.

- What kind of person are you looking for?
- What are your interests?
- What personal qualities do you like?
- How about looks?

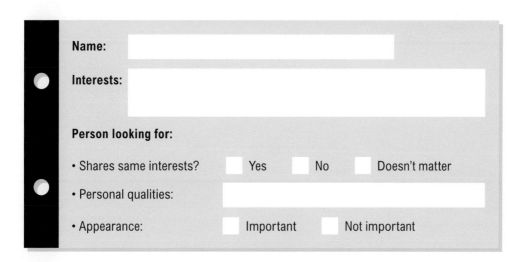

Celebrity lookalikes

Listen and fill in the following blanks to complete the passage. T-03

When someone _____ a crime, police generally ask for a
_____ of the criminal: age, _____ , hair color, visible
scars. Sometimes a police artist draws a picture _____ on the description
that is sent out to other police departments and the _____ . In a science
fiction novel by William Gibson, police get descriptions of _____ by asking
what famous _____ they look like. Witnesses might say someone looks like
"Mick Jagger with a _____ " or "a young Frank Sinatra."

1 **Complete the sentences using the words in the list.**

| blind date | anniversary | family reunion | reception | cousin | lose weight |

1. She met her husband on a _____.
2. At our _____ we meet long-lost relatives.
3. This diet is good for anyone who wants to _____.
4. Do you recognize my _____? He is wearing a bowtie and standing next to the bride.
5. We'll be celebrating our 20th wedding _____ soon.
6. They enjoyed a wonderful dinner at the wedding _____.

2 **A** **Listen and circle the names you hear.**

CD1 28

Paul / Tommy / Roger / Philip / Betsy / Bobby / Mark / Manny

B **Listen again and circle *T* for *True* or *F* for *False*.**

CD1 28

1. They can see Cousin Roger and Bobby over there.   T / F
2. Aunt Betsy looks old for her age.   T / F
3. They met on an online dating site.   T / F
4. The mother is easily moved to tears.   T / F
5. The bride's brother came from the Philippines.   T / F

C **Where are the speakers? Check (✓) the correct event.**

☐ family reunion   ☐ wedding   ☐ birthday party   ☐ office party

3

A **Listen to the conversation at a wedding reception. Where does each person live now? Match the people to the places. One place is extra.**

Aunt Gertrude •

Cousin Emily •

Uncle Morty •

Aunt Jean •

• Bermuda

• Chicago

• Atlantic City

• New York

• Boston

Listen for it

Gosh is an informal way of expressing mild surprise or delight.

B **Listen again and find the people. Match the names to the correct people (a–k).**

- **Cousin Emily** _____
- **Aunt Gertrude** _____
- **Aunt Jean** _____
- **Uncle Morty** _____

C Listen again and answer the following questions.

CD1
29

1. When did Rick see Peggy last time?

   _____

2. Why is Aunt Gertrude so thin now?

   Because _____.

3. Does Uncle Morty want to move out of New York?   Yes / No

4. With whom does Cousin Emily live in Bermuda?

   She lives with _____.

5. How old is Aunt Jean?   _____

4

A Listen to the conversation. Which of the cities is each person from? Write the city next to the person's name.

CD1
30

- **Bob Price**   _____
- **Nancy Jordan**   _____
- **Steve Maglieri**   _____

B Listen again and find the three people described. Match the names to the correct people (a–f).

CD1
30

- **Bob Price**   _____
- **Nancy Jordan**   _____
- **Steve Maglieri**   _____

5   **Listen and circle the correct response.**

1.   **a.** Yeah, doesn't she look well?
       b. Her name is Gertrude.
       c. Yes, there is.

2.   **a.** She does look young, doesn't she?
       b. She's looking at herself.
       c. I think she's 63 years old.

3.   **a.** I like him a lot.
       b. Yes, let's say hello.
       c. Yes, Morty has two suits.

4.   **a.** He's by the window.
       b. That's my brother, Leo.
       c. The one talking with my brothers?

5.   **a.** Yes, she's really good-looking.
       b. She's pretty young.
       c. Yes, I think that's Emily.

6.   **a.** His uncle's name is Joe.
       b. Yeah, Joe met my uncle.
       c. Yeah, I met him last year.

6   **A**   **Listen and match the person to the description.**

Rachel   •   • . . . has put on weight.

John   •   • . . . has a mustache.

Simon   •   • . . . has lost weight.

Fiona   •   • . . . looks friendly.

Frank   •   • . . . is pretty.

Judy   •   • . . . looks cute.

Tom   •   • . . . looks stylish.

B Listen again and find the people. Match the names to the correct people (a–k).

CD1
32

- Judy _____
- Rachel _____
- John _____
- Fiona _____
- Simon _____
- Tom _____
- Frank _____

Asking and talking about special events

Think of a family or friend event you attended. Make a conversation about it.

- Have you been to a family or friend event recently?
  — Yes, I have been to my _____ .
- What was it like?
  — Well, the wedding/reception/food was _____ .
- How many people turned up?
  — I guess around _____ .
- So, was it fun?

In Focus ## Crying in the chapel

Listen and fill in the following blanks to complete the passage. ● T-04

Is marriage obsolete? Since the 1950s, [1] _____ numbers of married couples
and [2] _____ divorce rates have led some to believe that it is. But huge
numbers of people continue to [3] _____ marriage as an important life goal,
and the vast majority will marry at least [4] _____ in their lifetime. One reason
people regard marriage so highly is that it can [5] _____ people with
a source of emotional [6] _____, mutual [7] _____, and
lasting [8] _____.

4 Asking and talking about school subjects

1 Complete the sentences using the words in the list. Be sure to use the correct form of the word.

architecture	weakness	register	advanced	grade	oxygen

1. It is important to know your own strengths and _____.
2. I like sports and my _____ in physical education is very good.
3. To study _____, strong mathematical ability is also important.
4. Water is a chemical compound made up of hydrogen and _____.
5. To _____ as a student you must pay tuition fees.
6. He is good at science and in the _____ class now.

2

A Listen to the three lessons. Which subjects are being taught? Number the subjects (1–3).

CD1 33 35

- Home Economics _____
- Mathematics _____
- History _____
- English _____
- Geography _____
- Computer Science _____
- Science _____
- Industrial Arts _____

B Listen again and answer the following questions.

CD1 33 35

1. When did the First World War start?

   _____

2. How many electrons does helium have?

   _____

3. Where does Roberta live?

   _____

3

A Listen to the two counseling interviews and complete the chart.

Listen for it

OK has many uses, for example, to begin a sentence, to show understanding, and to ask for or express acceptance.

	Student	Wants to be or do	Strengths	Weaknesses
1.	Jenny Tan			
2.	Julie Morris			

B Listen again and answer the following questions.

1. **a.** What is necessary to study architecture? _____

   b. What subject does Jenny have to study harder? _____

2. **a.** What career did the teacher first suggest to Julie? _____

   b. What does Julie seem to be interested in? _____

C Listen again and circle *T* for *True* or *F* for *False*.

1. **a.** Jenny has changed her career plans.   **T / F**

   b. Jenny is in the advanced math class.   **T / F**

2. **a.** Julie is not interested in computers.   **T / F**

   b. Julie will get some information about sports medicine. **T / F**

4 Listen and circle the correct response.

CD1
38

1. a. Not so good.
   b. It's pretty difficult.
   c. I like it.

2. a. Not so good.
   b. Not bad.
   c. No, not really.

3. a. Not really.
   b. Not bad.
   c. No, I don't like it.

4. a. Something with computers.
   b. When I'm eighteen.
   c. About 5:00 in the afternoon.

5. a. I guess so.
   b. Every day.
   c. Oh, the usual stuff.

6. a. Oh, languages, definitely.
   b. Yes, they are.
   c. I'm not very good at math.

5

A Listen and circle the best answer.

CD1
39

1. John is talking to . . .
   a. his dad.
   b. a teacher.
   c. an employer.

2. John's dad thinks he should . . .
   a. work with computers.
   b. study medicine.
   c. study languages.

3. John's dad is . . .
   a. a computer programmer.
   b. an engineer.
   c. a doctor.

4. They are talking about . . .
   a. John's grades.
   b. John's part-time job.
   c. John's future career.

B Listen again and complete the chart.

CD1
39

Name	Wants to be	Strengths	Weaknesses
John Lee			

6

A Listen to the descriptions of classes offered at a college and complete the chart. For "Class name," use the class names in the list.

CD1 40

Listen for it

A *high-flying* career means a very successful career.

Architectural Design   Computer Programming
Music Composition   Sports Medicine

Class name				
Instructor	Matt Harper	Ellen Carter	Carol Warren	Ben Keating
Classroom	447A		744C	
Class time	Tue–Fri 9 a.m.–12:30 p.m.	Mon–Thu 9 a.m.–3 p.m.		Wednesdays 1–5 p.m.

B Listen again and circle *T* for *True* or *F* for *False*.

CD1 40

1. Using the Automated Registration System, you can get information about programs, register for classes, and pay tuition fees.   **T / F**

2. The Music Composition course gives students the know-how to get a job in the recording industry.   **T / F**

3. The Sports Medicine course encourages elderly people to take care of their health.   **T / F**

4. One of the popular classes for Architectural Design is held on weekdays.   **T / F**

5. The Computer Programming course has three semesters.   **T / F**

C **Listen again and circle the best answer.**

1. Graduates from the Music Composition course have begun musical activities such as . . .
   a. playing for global bands on world tour.
   b. playing with local bands and beginning successful solo careers.
   c. beginning successful solo careers with top class players.

2. The instructor for the Music Composition course is . . .
   a. a guitarist.
   b. a pianist.
   c. a dancer.

3. Sports Medicine is aimed at students who . . .
   a. want to increase interest in fitness.
   b. are considering careers as teachers or coaches.
   c. are thinking about becoming medical doctors.

4. The Sports Medicine course has lectures on . . .
   a. health and welfare.
   b. medicine and biology.
   c. health and biology.

5. Architectural Design attracts students who are interested in . . .
   a. the latest architectural design.
   b. starting a high-flying career in the architectural industry.
   c. getting an outline of architectural engineering and design.

6. In the Computer Programming course, you can learn . . .
   a. basic knowledge to update your computer skills.
   b. how to start a successful career in the computer industry.
   c. how to become an entrepreneur in the computer industry.

Asking and talking about school subjects

Try this . . .

Imagine you are a career counselor for students. Interview your partner.

- What were your best subjects in high school?
  — My best subjects were _____ and _____.
- Which types of subjects interest you now?
  — I really enjoy _____.
- What sort of career are you interested in?
  — I'd like to be a(n) _____.
- Have you thought about working for _____?

In Focus Back to school

Listen and fill in the following blanks to complete the passage. ● T-05

For generations in the United States, a nineteenth century ⓿_____ known as the public school system was seen as the best way to give students the ❷_____ and skills to become productive ❸_____. Around the 1960s, experts began questioning the system, citing the need for new types of schools to meet the changing ❹_____ of the twentieth century. These reformers eventually ❺_____ for parents a much broader range of educational ❻_____—including ❼_____, alternative, and charter schools and home schooling—but they also sparked a ❽_____ on teaching and learning that still divides experts to this day.

1 **Complete the sentences using the words in the list.**

| ruined city | skyscrapers | gorge | safari | continent | volcano |

1. Australia is the largest island on earth, and the smallest _____.
2. When we go on a _____ in the desert, we like to cook on an open fire.
3. The guide took us on a day trip to the _____ of Machu Picchu.
4. The _____ erupted, raining hot ash over a wide area.
5. The tallest buildings in London are small in comparison with New York's

   _____.

6. We walked across a rope bridge over a _____.

2 **A** **Listen to the quiz program and circle the correct answer.**

CD1
41

1. Which is the highest mountain in the world?

   a. Mt. Fuji   **b.** Mt. Everest   **c.** K2

2. In which country can you find the Great Pyramid at Giza?

   a. Egypt   **b.** Mexico   **c.** Indonesia

3. What is the world's longest river?

   a. The Amazon   **b.** The Mississippi   **c.** The Nile

4. In which country can you find the ruined city of Machu Picchu?

   a. Brazil   **b.** Argentina   **c.** Peru

5. In which Japanese city can you find the world's oldest wooden temple?

   a. Kyoto   **b.** Nara   **c.** Tokyo

6. Which is the world's highest waterfall?

   a. Angel Falls, Venezuela

   b. Victoria Falls, Zimbabwe

   c. Niagara Falls, United States/Canada

7. Which skyscraper became the world's tallest building in 1998?

   a. Sears Tower, Chicago

   b. Petronas Towers, Kuala Lumpur

   c. Bank of China Tower, Hong Kong

8. The area near Tienhsiang in Taiwan is famous for which natural feature?

   a. A volcano   b. A gorge   c. A rain forest

9. Mammoth Cave National Park, the world's largest cave system, is in which U.S. state?

   a. Kentucky   b. North Dakota   c. California

10. South Korea's highest mountain is Mt. Halla, on Jeju Island. How high is it?

    a. 1,450 m   b. 1,950 m   c. 2,450 m

B **Listen again and fill in the following blanks.**

🎧 CD1 41

1. Mt. Everest is _____ meters high.

2. The Great Pyramid is _____ years old.

3. The world's longest river is _____ kilometers long.

4. Horyuji Temple is _____ years old.

5. Angel Falls is _____ meters high.

6. The twin Petronas Towers are _____ meters high.

7. The total length of the Mammoth Cave system is _____ kilometers.

3

A How does the speaker describe the places? Listen and circle the adjectives you hear.

CD1 42

incredible / amazing / stunning / awesome / unbelievable / spectacular / awe-inspiring / indescribable / beautiful / phenomenal

Listen for it

If something is *out of this world* it means it's amazing or unique.

B Listen again and circle *T* for *True* or *F* for *False*.

CD1 42

1. Three hundred years have passed since Mount Fuji erupted. **T / F**
2. In the rain forests of Brazil, there are various kinds of animals and birds. **T / F**
3. Niagara Falls is on the border of the United States and Canada. **T / F**
4. In Ayutthaya, there is a statue of Buddha covered in 200 kg of solid gold. **T / F**

4

A Listen. What is this announcement? Check (✓) the best answer.

CD1 43

☐ A weather report for Australia
☐ A travel ad for Australia
☐ A quiz show about Australia
☐ A news report about Australia
☐ A documentary about Australia

Listen for it

To *get away from it all* means to go somewhere far away and remote.

B Listen again and fill in the following blanks.

CD1 43

Australia is the _____ continent and the _____ island on earth. It's also the _____ country. The Great Barrier Reef is the _____ reef in the world. Uluru, or Ayer's Rock, is the world's _____ monolith.

5

Listen and trace Ed's route on the map.

Kakadu National Park

Great Barrier Reef

The Pinnacles

Sydney

Uluru

Melbourne

B

Listen again. Which of the places Ed visited was . . .

1. the most fun? _____
2. the most beautiful? _____
3. the most exciting? _____
4. the most unusual? _____

6   **Listen and circle the correct answer.**

CD1
45

1.   **a.**   Australia
    b.   Canada
    c.   Japan

3.   **a.**   North Africa
    b.   South America
    c.   Eastern Europe

5.   **a.**   The Indian Ocean
    b.   The Pacific Ocean
    c.   The Atlantic Ocean

2.   **a.**   Asia
    b.   Australia
    c.   Africa

4.   **a.**   Australia
    b.   The United States
    c.   Brazil

6.   **a.**   The Philippines
    b.   Denmark
    c.   Mexico

7   **A**   **Listen and circle *T* for *True* or *F* for *False*.**

CD1
46

1.	The man and the woman went to Australia together.	**T / F**
2.	Dave went to Australia on business.	**T / F**
3.	He enjoyed his trip.	**T / F**
4.	He went to the desert.	**T / F**
5.	When he was in Cairns, he stayed on a boat.	**T / F**
6.	He flew to Cape York.	**T / F**

B   **Listen again and draw Dave's route on the map.**

CD1
46

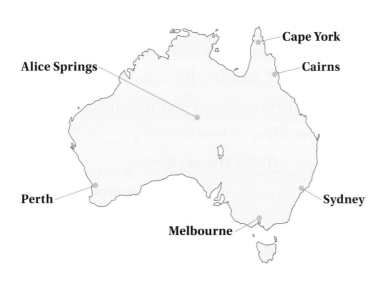

Your Turn!

Asking and talking about a trip

Try this . . .

Imagine you've just come back from a trip. Make a conversation about the trip.

- So, where did you go?
  — We took a trip to _____.
- How long did you go?
  — We went for _____.
- What did you do there?
- Did you enjoy your trip?

In Focus ▶ **The World Heritage List**

Listen and fill in the following blanks to complete the passage. T-06

The World Heritage List is a list of the most important natural and $_\text{①}$_____
sites around the world, compiled and updated $_\text{②}$_____ by the United Nations
Educational, Scientific, and Cultural Organization (UNESCO). In 2002, a total of 730 sites
were $_\text{③}$_____ on the list, including the Statue of Liberty in the United States,
Iguazú National Park in Argentina, the Great Barrier Reef in Australia, the Great Wall of China,
and the Acropolis in Athens, Greece. Many of these sites are $_\text{④}$_____ by
tourism and $_\text{⑤}$_____. UNESCO works for the $_\text{⑥}$_____ of each
of the sites on the list, to $_\text{⑦}$_____ that future generations may experience the
natural and cultural $_\text{⑧}$_____ we enjoy today.

1

Complete the sentences using the words in the list. Be sure to use the correct form of the word.

fix	advertisement	public transportation
convenient	ridiculous	renovation

1. The old Tudor-style home is in need of _____.

2. The museum is easily accessible by _____.

3. It is _____ to have the station so close.

4. The _____ will appear on the back cover of next week's *Time*.

5. I took my watch to be _____.

6. He laughed off her criticism as _____.

2

A **Listen to the conversation and circle the best answer.**

1. According to the advertisement, they can have . . .
   a. a full view of the harbor.
   b. a great view of the ocean.
   c. a great view of the metropolis.

2. Since the public transportation is so close, . . .
   a. they don't need a car.
   b. they can take a good walk for exercise.
   c. it's really convenient for doing some exercise.

3. The sports facilities are conveniently located . . .
   a. on the first floor.
   b. in the neighborhood.
   c. downstairs.

4. Second bedrooms are . . .
   a. always as big as the main bedroom.
   b. always bigger than the main bedroom.
   c. never as big as the main bedroom.

Listen again and circle *T* for *True* or *F* for *False*.

1. The front door needs to be repaired.   **T / F**
2. The apartment has a good view of the ocean.   **T / F**
3. There is a gym in the apartment building.   **T / F**
4. There is a shopping center nearby.   **T / F**
5. The second bedroom is spacious.   **T / F**

Listen for it

That's a plus is used informally to point out a positive aspect of a thing or situation.

C **Listen again. Make a list of the good points (pros) and bad points (cons) of the apartment.**

	Pros	Cons
1.		
2.		
3.		

3 **Listen and circle the best response.**

1. a. But I always drive to work.
   b. But I don't own a car.

4. a. You can use the one next door.
   b. The rent is eight hundred a month.

2. a. It's really convenient.
   b. You can see it from the back.

5. a. We'll get it fixed.
   b. But it's very small.

3. a. It looks kind of small to me.
   b. It needs to be fixed.

You will hear descriptions of three luxury homes. Match the description of each home to the correct celebrity owner.

1.

Beautiful
2-story Tudor-style house

- 4,700 square ft.
- 4 bdrm, 5 bthrm, 3-car garage
- swimming pool, patio, putting green
- location: Encino, California

Price: US$

2.

Stunning
4-story Georgian mansion

- central London location
- 6 bdrm, 5 bthrm
- library, sweeping staircase
- separate servants' apartment

Price: US$

3.

Spectacular
2-story mansion

- 9,000 square ft., close to Sunset Blvd.
- 5 bdrm, 6 1/2 bthrm
- master suite incl. gym, outdoor terrace
- garden with pools, patios, waterfall

Price: US$

Frank Sinatra

Madonna

Samuel L. Jackson

B **What is the asking price for each property? Listen again and fill in the price.**

C **Listen again and circle *T* for *True* or *F* for *False*.**

1. With several changes to the home's exterior, a pool, a patio, and a garage were added to the Tudor-style home.   **T / F**

2. The house which used to be owned by Madonna is in an exclusive residential district in London.   **T / F**

3. The house owned by Frank Sinatra has the master suite on the first floor.   **T / F**

1. The _____ home on our _____ covers 4,700 square feet. The owner purchased this Tudor-style home in _____ and has since made a number of _____.

2. This four-story mansion is suitable for a newly _____ couple. If you're looking for a _____ starter home and planning a big family, there's no better _____. The mansion is located in one of the most _____ addresses in London.

3. The master suite _____ up the entire _____ floor—_____ with two bathrooms, a dressing room, a gym, and an outdoor terrace. The best feature of this mansion is the massive _____ kitchen where the former owner cooked Italian _____.

5 **Listen and circle the correct response.**

1. a. It's not too far.
   b. The subway closes at 11.
   c. It's close to the park.

2. a. There are three bathrooms.
   b. Two large ones.
   c. In the basement.

3. a. I don't think so.
   b. Yes, you can play pool.
   c. That's true, but the sea is nearby.

4. a. I'd like a sea view.
   b. That's OK.
   c. You can see the ocean from the back.

5. a. Yes, it's quite small.
   b. Yes, it's quite big.
   c. It could be, I guess.

6. a. We'll have it fixed.
   b. It's in front of the house.
   c. I'm glad to hear that.

CD1
57

A **Listen and circle *T* for *True*, *F* for *False*, or *U* for *Unknown*.**

1. Helen is talking to a real estate agent. **T / F / U**
2. She is looking for a three-bedroom apartment. **T / F / U**
3. The rent is more than $1,000 a month. **T / F / U**
4. She wants a place that's quiet. **T / F / U**
5. She decides to look at an apartment. **T / F / U**
6. She decides to rent the place. **T / F / U**

B **Listen again and circle the best answer.**

CD1
57

1. Did Helen have any particular neighborhood in mind?
   a. Yes, she did.
   b. No, she didn't.

2. She just wants to live in a place close to . . .
   a. public transportation.
   b. a shopping center.

3. She can see the ocean . . .
   a. from the back.
   b. in front of the apartment house.

4. They will meet at . . . o'clock.
   a. three
   b. five

C **Listen again. Which place are they talking about? Circle the correct ad.**

CD1
57

Apartments for Rent

a. **Two Bedroom Apt.**
Spacious two-bedroom with balcony. Situated right in the heart of downtown city area. High floor, across from shopping mall. Near train station. Tel: 555-9967.

b. **Fully Furnished Apt.**
Fully furnished three-bedroom apt. for rent. Steps from university, public transportation. Avail. Dec 10th. Affordable rent. Call Jim at 555-3598.

c. **Convenient Location**
Conveniently located two-bedroom apt. for lease. Quiet suburban neighborhood, close to beach and major bus routes. Full facilities, sea views. Call 555-6298.

Your Turn!

Asking about and describing homes

Try this . . .

Imagine you're a real estate agent for the stars. Your partner is a celebrity looking for a new home. Describe one of the homes in Task 4 (or make up your own information) and answer your partner's questions. Switch roles and make notes.

- How many rooms does it have?
- Does it have a swimming pool?
- How many cars does the garage hold?
- How is the view from the house?

In Focus **Dream homes**

Listen and fill in the following blanks to complete the passage. T-07

In 1919, multi-[1]_____ publisher William Randolph Hearst decided to do something with a huge tract of [2]_____ in California he had [3]_____ from his mother. "We are tired of [4]_____ out in the open at the ranch in San Simeon," Hearst is said to have written. "I would like to build a little something." Years and millions of dollars later, that "little something" turned out to be Hearst Castle, a 165-bedroom mansion that [5]_____ a marble and 22-carat-gold swimming pool, 1,000-year-old artifacts, and even its own zoo. Hearst may never have been [6]_____ with his dream home—he made countless [7]_____— but tourists still flock to the castle to [8]_____ at its spectacular grandeur.

44

1

Complete the sentences using the words in the list.

guarantee	genuine	jewelry	budget	discount	fake

1. The _____ was so perfect that even the experts didn't realize that it wasn't a real Stradivarius.
2. I had all my _____ stolen.
3. Customers are offered a 10% _____ if they pay cash.
4. On closer examination, it was found to be a _____ diamond.
5. Congress cut $10 billion from the _____.
6. There is a one-year _____ on this computer.

2

A **Listen to the three conversations. What are the people trying to sell? Number the items (1–3).**

CD1 58 ▼ 60

- wristwatch _____
- sunglasses _____
- cell phone _____

Listen for it

Look is sometimes used to interrupt someone or encourage the person to pay close attention to what you're about to say.

B **Listen again and fill in the following blanks.**

CD1 58 ▼ 60

1. At the mall you'll pay _____ for a pair of sunglasses.
2. At the store it costs _____ and comes with a guarantee.
3. The woman wants to wear it to tell _____.

3

A   **Listen to the conversation and number the sentences (1–7) in the order you hear them.**

- I won't pay more than $50.   _____
- Have you got anything cheaper?   _____
- Would you take $40?   _____
- You can't lower the price at all?   _____
- What if I buy two?   _____
- Could you give me a discount?   _____
- Sorry, that's too much.   _____

B   **Listen again and circle the best answer.**

1. Peter wants to buy . . . for his girlfriend.
      a. a gold necklace   **b.** a silver necklace   **c.** a silver bracelet

2. Peter cannot pay more than . . . for the jewelry.
      a. $40   **b.** $50   **c.** $60

3. Does the salesgirl eventually agree with the price offered by Peter?   Yes / No

4. How many necklaces does Peter buy?   One / Two

5. How much do they cost in total? $50 / $100

4   **Listen and circle the best response.**

1. **a.** No, thanks. I'm not interested.
      b. No, thanks. They're not silk.
      c. No, thanks. I'm not wearing a watch.

2. **a.** Thanks, but I don't wear them.
      b. Thanks, but I don't take them.
      c. No thanks. Could you give me a discount?

3. **a.** I have a CD player.

   b. I'll give you twelve fifty.

   c. Sorry, that's too much.

4. **a.** Could you give me a discount?

   b. Could you give me fifty dollars?

   c. Could you give me your last CD?

5. **a.** I don't need it quickly.

   b. I don't need a bike.

   c. I don't need to sell it.

6. **a.** What if I buy two?

   b. Would you take four fifty?

   c. Do you have any ties?

A **Listen and circle *T* for *True*, *F* for *False*, or *U* for *Unknown*.**

CD1
68

1. Lisa is speaking to a salesgirl.   T / F / U
2. Lisa arrives late.   T / F / U
3. They are in a restaurant.   T / F / U
4. Lisa met a man selling stuff.   T / F / U
5. Lisa knew the watch was not genuine.   T / F / U

Listen for it

Stuff is a general term used informally to refer to unspecified items or objects.

B **Listen again and answer the following questions.**

CD1
68

1. What was Lisa doing just before she arrived?

   _____

2. What does the other person think of the goods being sold on Bonham Road?

   _____

3. What does the other person think of what Lisa bought?

   _____

4. What might Lisa have to do with her purchase?

   _____

6 Listen and circle the correct response.

1. a. I can make it cheaper.
    b. But it looks genuine.
    c. I already have one.

2. a. Thanks, but I don't wear them.
    b. Thanks, but I don't use them.
    c. I already have a suit.

3. a. Do they work?
    b. How much are they?
    c. Are they genuine silk?

4. a. Can I pay by credit card?
    b. Not much.
    c. I bought six pens.

5. a. What's your best price?
    b. I don't wear them.
    c. I can give you a great price.

6. a. Do you like jewelry?
    b. That's too much.
    c. I can give you a special price.

7 **A** Listen and fill in the following blanks.

1. Jenny has been _____.
2. She paid _____ for each item.
3. Tonight, she's going to a _____.

B Listen again and circle the best answer.

1. Jenny thinks what she bought are . . .
    a. expensive.
    b. reasonable in price.
    c. a real bargain.

2. What she bought feels like . . .
    a. genuine wool.
    b. genuine silk.
    c. fake silk.

3. What she bought will match . . .
    a. her new jeans.
    b. her new sweater.
    c. her new dress.

C **Listen again. Which item will Jenny have/wear tonight? Check (✓) the correct item.**

CD1
70

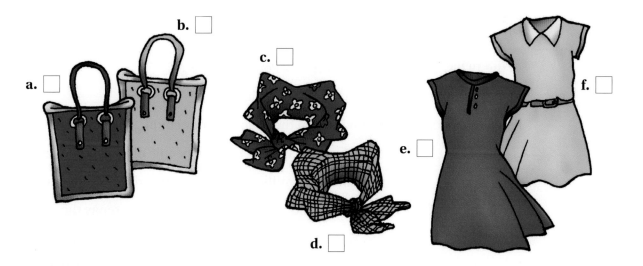

b. ☐
c. ☐
a. ☐
f. ☐
e. ☐
d. ☐

Your Turn!

Discussing and bargaining for consumer goods

Try this . . .

Imagine you are a salesperson. Write the names of three different consumer goods that you want to sell. List an asking price and note details for each. Negotiate until your partner agrees to buy what you are selling. Switch roles.

- Looking for a gift, sir/madam? Take a look at this.

  — That looks good. How much is it?

- This bracelet is just $_____.

  — Could you give me a discount?

- This is top quality. Look at these features.

  — Thanks, but I don't need it.

- I can let you have the bracelet for $_____.

  — OK. It's a deal.

Too good to be true

Listen and fill in the following blanks to complete the passage.　T-08

In the 1920s, small-time crook Charles Ponzi began a (1)_____ scheme that made him America's most infamous swindler. The (2)_____ was simple: Ponzi told people that by giving him their money, they could (3)_____ their (4)_____ in just 45 days. Over 10,000 people did so and Ponzi soon (5)_____ almost $10 million. What investors didn't know was that Ponzi was taking money from the second round of investors and using it to repay the (6)_____. He used the remaining (7)_____ to bankroll his lavish lifestyle. Predictably, Ponzi soon ran out of takers and was unable to repay all of his investors. Ponzi's scheme—for which he was sent to (8)_____—helped popularize the saying, "If something looks too good to be true, it probably is."

1 Complete the sentences using the words in the list. Be sure to use the correct form of the word.

| weird | complain | satisfaction | vet | load | certificate |

1. There was a _____ atmosphere in the antique shop.
2. She _____ to me that the book was too difficult for her.
3. There were many tankers _____ and unloading.
4. The _____ says that he is a qualified mechanic.
5. I've got to take the dog to the _____'s tomorrow.
6. The survey indicates that job _____ has fallen to its lowest level.

2 **A** Listen. Who is talking? Write the occupation of the first person in each conversation.

CD1 71 ▾ 73

1. _____
2. _____
3. _____

B Listen again and circle *T* for *True* or *F* for *False*.

CD1 71 ▾ 73

1. **a.** The patient has had pain for about two weeks.   T / F
   b. He is in good health.   T / F

2. **a.** Both of the customers are ready to order their food.   T / F
   b. The waiter helps them decide what they should order.   T / F

3. **a.** The total cost is $19.86.   T / F
   b. The customer pays in cash.   T / F

3

CD1
74
77

A Listen and circle the statement that is closest in meaning to what each person says. What do these people do? Write the occupations.

Listen for it

Weird is an informal way of saying *strange* or *unusual*.

	Statement	Occupation
1.	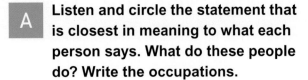 **a.** A lot of women want to do this job. **b.** Very few women do this kind of work.	
2.	**a.** The worst thing about my job is having to get up early. **b.** I don't like being on TV.	
3.	**a.** My job is terrible, because my manager is always complaining. **b.** I don't like it when customers are dissatisfied.	
4.	**a.** I get satisfaction from helping people to be successful. **b.** My former students are all successful.	

B Listen again and complete the following scripts.

CD1
74
77

1. I guess lots of people think I have a really _____ job.

2. I get to _____ people, and everybody _____ watches the morning news on TV knows _____ I am.

3. I hate it when people come back and _____. They usually say that the shoes don't _____ right, or that they _____ too much.

4. . . . they say that I helped them to reach their _____ in life. I mean, . . . Job _____ is more important than money.

4

A   **Listen and write the correct name (Nick, Jim, or Linda) to complete each sentence.**

CD1
78

1. _____ doesn't want to have a pet.

2. _____ wants to be a teacher.

3. _____ had a really cool job.

4. _____ cleaned as part of the job.

5. _____ wore a winter coat at work.

B   **Listen again and circle the best answer.**

CD1
78

1. What did Nick do?

    a. He worked for the local veterinarian.

    b. He worked at the local hospital.

    c. He did some voluntary work at the local hospital.

2. Why doesn't Nick want to have a pet?

    a. Because he does not want to take care of animals.

    b. Because he saw what went wrong with the animals.

    c. Because he cannot save sick animals.

3. Where did Jim work?

    a. At a frozen food company

    b. At a transport company

    c. In a home delivery service

4. Where did Linda work?

    a. At a kindergarten

    b. At a child care center

    c. At a home for the aged

5. What does she want to do?

    a. Take care of elderly people

    b. Serve as a health-care worker

    c. Teach young children

 5   **Listen and circle the correct response.**

1.   **a.** I had a part-time job.

    b. I prefer working outdoors.

    c. I love summer.

2.   **a.** It's kind of boring.

    b. Working with people.

    c. Any job can be interesting.

3.   **a.** Something part-time.

    b. I look at the ads in the newspaper.

    c. I'm working at the local pool.

4.   **a.** It's interesting.

    b. Something part-time.

    c. Oh, job satisfaction.

5.   **a.** Preferably weekends.

    b. Definitely.

    c. I work with a lot of people.

6.   **a.** Something part-time.

    b. I enjoy my weekend job.

    c. I'd prefer evenings.

 6   **A**   **Listen and circle the best answer.**

1. What would Jake like to do?

    a. Work in a school

    b. Find a full-time job

    c. Find a part-time job

2. How many jobs are mentioned?

    a. Two

    b. Three

    c. Four

3. What kind of work was suggested first?

    a. Restocking the shelves at a supermarket

    b. Restocking the storage place at a shop

    c. Checking the stock at a shop

4. Which job is Jake interested in?

    a. The supermarket job

    b. The lifeguard job

    c. He is not interested in any of the jobs.

5. What does Jake need to work at the local pool?

    a. A bodyguard's certificate

    b. A teaching certificate

    c. A lifeguard's certificate

B **Listen again and fill in the form.**

CD1
80

Job Search Details

Name:	Jake Campbell		
Current employment:	☐ student	☐ self-employed	☐ employee
Preferred hours:	☐ weekdays	☐ evenings	☐ weekends
Preferred location:	☐ indoor	☐ outdoor	☐ doesn't matter
Prefers working with people?	☐ yes	☐ no	☐ doesn't matter
Any qualifications?			

Your Turn!

Asking about and describing jobs

Try this . . .

Describe your job and answer your partner's questions.

- Do you have a part-time job?
- What do you do?
  — I work as a sales clerk in a pizza shop.
- About how much does the job pay?
  — _____ yen per hour.
- Do you enjoy working with other people?

In Focus ## Someone's got to do it . . .

Listen and fill in the following blanks to complete the passage. ● T-09

Wanted: Three people to sniff armpits. Must have a good nose. Easy work for good pay.

Think this is a ❶_____? Jobs like this are actually offered by companies that

make deodorants and other personal hygiene ❷_____. When

❸_____ in the hygiene industry develop deodorants with new and different

❹_____, they have to determine which ones the public likes best. They

typically have around twenty ❺_____ men ❻_____ different

formulas to their underarms and then subject their armpits to an ❼_____

inspection—not with the eyes but with the ❽_____. That's where the armpit-

sniffers come in. Yes, it's a smelly job, but somebody has to do it. It could be you!

1 Complete the sentences using the words in the list. Be sure to use the correct form of the word.

| photocopy | reconfirm | aisle seat | itinerary | pharmacy | waste |

1. Would you pick up my medicine at the _____?

2. Which would you like, an _____ or a window seat?

3. According to our _____, we will arrive in Hong Kong in three hours.

4. It's a sin to _____ food when others do not have enough to eat.

5. Send us the _____ and keep the original.

6. He _____ his reservation on the morning flight.

2

A Listen and number the pictures (1–5). One is extra.

Listen for it

If something or someone is *due any second*, it means the event will happen or the person will arrive very soon.

B Listen again and circle *D* for *Done* or *IP* for *In progress* for each task.

1. D / IP   2. D / IP   3. D / IP   4. D / IP   5. D / IP

3 Listen and circle the correct response.

1. a. Yes, I did.
   b. Yes, I will.

2. a. The store was closed.
   b. Yes, I will.

3. a. The line was busy.
   b. Yes, he did.

4. a. Yes, she did.
   b. She wasn't in.

5. a. Yes, I will.
   b. No, I didn't.

6. a. I'm just checking.
   b. It's on your desk.

4

A Listen. Check (✓) the things Sandy needs to do.

☐ call airline
☐ put sweater in bag
☐ get extra cash from ATM

☐ cancel newspaper
☐ buy some medicine
☐ call the man's mother

☐ reconfirm flight
☐ book taxi

B Listen again. What is happening at these times? Fill in the planner.

3:30
_____

4:00
_____

5:30
_____

5

A Listen to Jenny's voice mail and check (✓) the things her boss asks her to do.

CD2
14

☐ reconfirm flight   ☐ change flight
☐ reserve aisle seat   ☐ get file
☐ copy speech   ☐ print out itinerary
☐ call boss's wife   ☐ send fax to boss's wife
☐ call a doctor for boss   ☐ send assistant to pharmacy

Listen for it

Mess up is an informal way of saying "make a mistake."

B Listen again and circle *T* for *True* or *F* for *False*.

CD2
14

1. Her boss is going to Seoul.   **T / F**
2. He has to give a speech.   **T / F**
3. His wife is going with him.   **T / F**
4. He is staying in a hotel.   **T / F**
5. He needs to take along his medicine.   **T / F**
6. His wife's name is Connie.   **T / F**

C Listen again and answer the following questions.

CD2
14

1. What mistake did the airline make last time?

_____

2. Where is the file?

_____

3. What doesn't he want to do in Seoul?

_____

6

☐ reconfirm flight   ☐ reserve aisle seat   ☐ make copies of speech
☐ fax itinerary to wife   ☐ pick up medicine

B **Listen again and circle the best answer.**

1. What seat could she get?

   a. A window seat

   b. An aisle seat

   c. A middle seat

2. What is she going to do tomorrow?

   a. Fix the fax machine

   b. Send the fax to the boss's wife

   c. Contact the boss's wife in Seoul

3. What does the boss ask her to do?

   a. Fax the itinerary to his Seoul hotel

   b. Explain the details about the machine's problem

   c. Call his wife and give her his hotel information

4. Did Connie pick up the medicine?

   a. Yes, she did.

   b. No, she didn't.

   c. She is picking up the medicine now.

5. What does the boss need to do?

   a. Pick up the medicine by himself

   b. Ask someone else to pick up the medicine

   c. Leave without the medicine

C **Listen again and answer the following questions.**

CD2
15

1. If the boss's wife cannot contact him, what will happen?

_____

2. Why couldn't Connie pick up the medicine?

_____

7

A **Listen and circle the best answer.**

CD2
16

1. This is . . .
    a. a telephone conversation.
    b. an answering machine message.
    c. a public announcement.

2. The person talking is . . .
    a. Jenny's husband.
    b. Jenny's boss.
    c. Jenny's coworker.

3. The person asks Jenny to . . .
    a. do some things for him.
    b. do some things for her boss.
    c. do some things for her husband.

B **Listen again. Check (✓) the things Jenny has to do tonight.**

CD2
16

☐ collect medicine from pharmacy
☐ send some faxes
☐ buy food for dinner
☐ buy a new fridge
☐ reserve a hotel room
☐ make a phone call
☐ reserve a seat at a restaurant
☐ pick up dry cleaning
☐ reserve a flight

Asking for information and making excuses

Imagine your partner works for you. Make a list of things your partner was supposed to do for you yesterday but didn't. Find out why these tasks weren't done. Switch roles.

- Did you do everything on the list yesterday?
- Did you print out my itinerary?
- What about the calls I asked you to make?
- Why didn't you send these faxes?

In Focus ## Houston, we have a problem

Listen and fill in the following blanks to complete the passage. ● T-10

Few would deny that technology has brought huge **(1)**_____ to humanity in terms of better health, improved **(2)**_____, and a better quality of life for millions. Without **(3)**_____ in medical technology, we might never have found cures for once dreaded **(4)**_____ like polio and tuberculosis. Without breakthroughs in engineering, we might never have reached outer space or even **(5)**_____ the skies. But what about the other side of the issue? Some experts claim that the ill effects of our growing **(6)**_____ on technology could actually **(7)**_____ the positive results. As examples, they typically cite the toll on the environment often attributed to the rise in the use of the automobile, and the **(8)**_____ of community and literacy resulting from the introduction of television.

Unit

10 Asking for and giving tour information

1 Complete the sentences using the words in the list.

ceiling	landmark	observation deck
architectural	cultural	cathedral

1. St. Patrick's _____ looks like a European church from the Middle Ages.

2. A chandelier hung from the _____.

3. An _____ lets you enjoy the view of the whole city.

4. The Statue of Liberty is the most famous _____ in New York City.

5. This church is one of the many _____ wonders in London.

6. It was a misunderstanding arising from different _____ beliefs.

2 **A** Listen to the three conversations. Which places are the people talking about? Number the places (1–3). One is extra.

Statue of Liberty

St. Patrick's Cathedral

Empire State Building

Grand Central Station

B Listen again and fill in the following blanks.

1. The _____ is painted so it looks like the sky at night.

2. The Statue of Liberty was originally brought to the United States in _____ pieces and rebuilt, and the whole thing weighs about _____ tons.

3. There are two observation decks—one on the _____th floor, and one on the _____ floor.

3

A Listen to the conversation and circle *T* for *True* or *F* for *False*.

1. Cindy works for a tour operator.   T / F
2. Both tours take three hours.   T / F
3. The Architectural Tour is in the morning.   T / F
4. They will have a coffee break at Barnes and Noble Bookstore.   T / F
5. The woman plans to take a tour next week.   T / F
6. The woman decides on the afternoon tour.   T / F

B Listen again and write *A* for places on the Architectural Tour and *C* for places on the Cultural Tour.

- **Empire State Building**   ____
- **Guggenheim Museum**   ____
- **St. Patrick's Cathedral**   ____
- **Central Park Zoo**   ____
- **Chrysler Building**   ____
- **Barnes and Noble Bookstore** ____
- **Carnegie Hall**   ____
- **Rockefeller Center**   ____
- **Grand Central Station**   ____

Listen for it

Ends up at . . . is another way to say *finishes at . . .*

A Listen to the guide describing a tour of Sydney. Which places are included on today's tour? Check (✓) them.

CD2
21

☐ Olympic Site ☐ Centrepoint Tower ☐ Opera House
☐ The Rocks ☐ Darling Harbour ☐ Paddington
☐ Botany Bay ☐ Royal Botanic Gardens ☐ Harbour Bridge
☐ Chinatown ☐ Bondi Beach

B Listen again. Where and at what time does *tomorrow*'s tour start? Where and when does it finish?

CD2
21

■ **Starting time:** _____ **Place:** _____
■ **Finishing time:** _____ **Place:** _____

C Listen again and circle the best answer.

CD2
21

1. At the Opera House they will look around . . .
   a. outside. **b.** inside.

2. At Bondi Beach what are they planning to do?
   a. Swim **b.** Fish

3. From the top of Centrepoint Tower what are they going to watch?
   a. The sunrise **b.** The sunset

4. At Darling Harbour they are going to . . .
   a. gamble. **b.** join the races.

5. What time is tomorrow's dinner?
   a. 6 p.m. **b.** 9 p.m.

5

A A tour guide is describing a tour through New York. Listen and draw the route on the map.

CD2 22

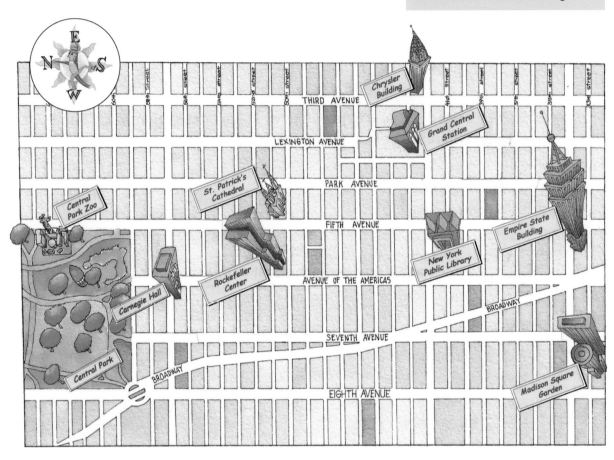

B Listen again and answer the following questions.

CD2 22

1. How long will they stay at the Central Park Zoo?
2. What does St. Patrick's Cathedral look like?
3. When did they start to build Rockefeller Center?
4. How long did it take to construct Grand Central Station?

6

A **Listen and circle the best answer.**

CD2
23

1. The man and woman are . . .
   a. friends.
   b. husband and wife.
   c. brother and sister.

2. How long are they staying in Paris?
   a. Two days
   b. Five days
   c. Seven days

3. The woman has seen a lot of pictures of . . .
   a. the Eiffel Tower.
   b. the Arc de Triomphe.
   c. the Louvre.

4. What can they see at Montmartre?
   a. Notre Dame Cathedral
   b. The Louvre
   c. The Sacre-Couer

5. What are they NOT planning to do tomorrow?
   a. See a dance show
   b. Climb the Eiffel Tower
   c. Visit a church

B **Listen again and circle *T* for *True* or *F* for *False*.**

CD2
23

1. They are visiting Paris on business.   **T / F**
2. They have stayed in Paris for five days.   **T / F**
3. The Louvre is not far from the Arc de Triomphe.   **T / F**
4. They have no time to go to the Sacre-Couer today.   **T / F**
5. They are going to see Notre Dame Cathedral tomorrow.   **T / F**

Asking for and giving tour information

Use the map on page 66. Plan a tour. Ask your partner about the tour and answer the questions.

- What kind of tour are you going to take?
- Where does your tour start?
- What are you going to see along the way?
  — We'll stop off at _____.
- Where does the tour finish?

In Focus A landmark remembered

Listen and fill in the following blanks to complete the passage.   T-11

Few people will forget where they were when they heard the news of the World Trade Center attack on September 11th, ❶ _____. Completed in ❷ _____, the twin towers of the World Trade Center were one of the most recognizable landmarks in the New York City skyline. Designed by Japanese-American architect Minoru Yamasaki, the WTC was the highest ❸ _____ in New York, a giant steel, concrete, and glass structure with ❹ _____ floors in each tower and more than

❺ _____ million square feet of office space. Yamasaki hoped his most famous creation would become "a living symbol of man's ❻ _____ to world peace;" although now ❼ _____, the symbol lives on in people's ❽ _____. The World Trade Center attack shocked people around the world.

1

Complete the sentences using the words in the list.

| authentic order allergic reservation delivery portion |

1. He's _____ to pollen and suffers from hay fever.
2. We have a special offer. We won't charge you for _____.
3. I'd like to place an _____ for ten copies of this book.
4. You need to use fresh herbs to get an _____ Italian taste.
5. I'll call the restaurant and make a _____.
6. Since she was very hungry, she ate a double _____ of the food.

2

A **Listen to the radio ads. Complete the ads with the restaurant addresses and phone numbers.**

CD2
24
26

Listen for it

Pull up a chair is an informal way of inviting someone to join you.

1.

Ole Mexican Restaurant
★★★
Authentic Mexican Food

Super value meals and best quality service.
Find us at:

_____
_____

Tel: _____

2.

Roma Café
Old-Style Italian Eatery

"Pasta and Pizza like Mamma used to make!"
Conveniently located at:

_____
_____

Tel: _____

3.

DRAGON CITY
City's #1 Chinese Buffet

as Voted by the Editors of
Dinning Out magazine
Location:

_____
_____

Tel: _____

B   Listen again and match the restaurants to the correct foods.

Ole Mexican Restaurant   •   •   spicy stir-fry dishes / sweet and sour dishes

Roma Café   •   •   pasta / meat / seafood dishes

Dragon City   •   •   fajitas / burritos / tacos / enchiladas

C   Listen again and complete the following scripts.

1.   . . . Ole Mexican Restaurant is home to the area's most _____ Mexican food. . . .

2.   . . . You'll find all the _____ dishes you're looking for at Roma Café. . . .

3.   . . . With an endless variety of dishes in its all-you-can-eat _____, Dragon City has something for every _____ . . .

3   Listen and circle the best response.

1.   **a.**   Sure. How much is it?
     b.   Sure. Are you ready to order?
     c.   Sure. What would you like?

2.   **a.**   No, just chicken and pork.
     b.   Chicken or pork?
     c.   There's chicken in it.

3.   **a.**   Do you have any soup?
     b.   How's the soup?
     c.   Would you like anything else?

4.   **a.**   Just vegetables.
     b.   Stir-fried and steamed.
     c.   Do you like vegetables?

5.   **a.**   Five of them.
     b.   Five dollars.
     c.   Table for five?

A Look at the menu and listen to the conversation. Check (✓) the items Joe and Margaret ordered.

CD2
32

Wong's Chinese Restaurant

Soups

Corn Soup ⋯⋯⋯⋯⋯ $1.50

Hot & Sour Soup ⋯⋯⋯ $2.00

Wonton Soup ⋯⋯⋯⋯ $1.50

Seafood

Garlic Prawns ⋯⋯⋯⋯ $5.00

Steamed Lobster ⋯⋯⋯ $6.00

Fried Fish ⋯⋯⋯⋯⋯⋯ $4.50

Steamed Fish ⋯⋯⋯⋯ $5.00

Meat Dishes

Lemon Chicken ⋯⋯⋯⋯ $4.50

Beef with Broccoli ⋯⋯ $5.50

Beef in Oyster Sauce ⋯ $5.00

Sweet & Sour Pork ⋯⋯ $5.00

Roasted Pork ⋯⋯⋯⋯ $4.50

Lamb w. Green Onions ⋯ $5.00

Chinese Dumplings

Various kinds from ⋯⋯ $1.50

Vegetable Dishes

Stir-fried Vegetables ⋯⋯ $3.50

Steamed Vegetables ⋯⋯ $3.50

Rice & Noodles

Steamed Rice ⋯⋯⋯⋯ $2.00

Fried Rice ⋯⋯⋯⋯⋯ $3.50

Fried Noodles ⋯⋯⋯⋯ $3.00

Drinks

Hot Tea ⋯⋯⋯⋯⋯⋯ $0.50

Soft Drinks ⋯⋯⋯⋯⋯ $1.00

B Listen again and circle the best answer.

CD2
32

1. Why did they decide to get take-out?

   a. They only had a frozen pizza.   **b.** The frozen pizza had been eaten.

2. How many orders of rice are they going to get?

   a. One   **b.** Two

C Listen again and check your answers. How much will they have to pay?

CD2
32

Listen for it

That should do it is an informal way of saying you don't need anything else.

$_____

5

A Look at the menu in Task 4 and listen to the conversation. Circle the items Joe and Margaret received.

B Listen again and circle *T* for *True*, *F* for *False*, or *U* for *Unknown*.

1. Joe ordered sweet and sour pork.   **T / F / U**
2. Margaret is allergic to lobster.   **T / F / U**
3. Joe does not eat lamb.   **T / F / U**
4. Margaret will just eat the steamed rice.   **T / F / U**
5. They are going to eat out instead.   **T / F / U**

C Listen again and circle the best answer.

1. What kind of dish is Margaret allergic to?
   a. Lobster
   b. Pork

2. What kind of rice dish did they receive?
   a. Fried Rice
   b. None

6

Listen and circle the correct response.

1. a. Yes, something to eat.
   b. Why? Are you hungry?
   c. I can't decide.

2. a. It's a kind of seafood.
   b. It's 25 dollars.
   c. No thanks, I'm allergic to it.

3. a. No, I prefer it steamed.
   b. It's very cheap.
   c. No, I prefer it fried.

4. a. Fried noodles.
   b. That's right.
   c. I think it is.

5. a. Now, that's one thing I love.
   b. Sure, here's a fork.
   c. Oh, I love sweet desserts.

6. a. Yes, I do.
   b. No, I don't.
   c. I like them both.

7

A **Listen and circle the best answer.**

1. The woman is . . .

   a. ordering at a restaurant.   **b.** ordering take-out.   **c.** ordering dessert.

2. How many dishes are mentioned?

   a. Five   **b.** Six   **c.** Seven

3. How many people is the woman ordering for?

   a. One   **b.** Three   **c.** Four

4. They have run out of . . .

   a. sweets.   **b.** sweet and sour pork.   **c.** ginger chicken.

B **Listen again and write the number of portions next to each dish the woman orders.**

Wong's Chinese Restaurant

Prices per individual portion

Meat

_____ red roast pork ·········· $5.50

_____ ginger chicken ·········· $5.80

_____ honey-glazed chicken ····· $5.30

_____ sweet and sour pork ····· $4.80

_____ barbecued duck ·········· $6.30

Seafood

_____ stir-fried shrimp ·········· $6.80

_____ steamed lobster ·········· $7.20

Rice and vegetables

_____ steamed rice ·········· $1.80

_____ fried rice ·········· $3.50

_____ stir-fried vegetables ······· $5.00

Your Turn!

Placing and taking orders for take-out food

Try this . . .

Use the menu in Task 4. Work with a partner. Take turns being an employee of Wong's Chinese Restaurant and a customer phoning to place a food order for delivery. Note your partner's order.

- Wong's Chinese Restaurant, how may I help you?
  — I'd like to place an order for delivery, please.
- Could you give me two orders of rice, please?
  — Sure. Would you like steamed or fried rice?

In Focus **Is meat murder?**

Listen and fill in the following blanks to complete the passage. ● T-12

Just as in the animal kingdom of carnivores, omnivores, and herbivores, humanity can be

❶ _____ into those who eat meat and those who don't. The broad term for people

who don't eat meat is vegetarian, but there are differences in eating ❷ _____ even

among the members of this group. Some people call themselves vegetarians because they

❸ _____ red meat, mainly beef. Others choose not to eat any kind of fish or meat.

Strict vegetarians, sometimes called "vegans," also ❹ _____ not to eat animal

products like eggs or ❺ _____ foods. Why do people become vegetarians? Some

do it out of ❻ _____ for their health, some because of their religious

❼ _____, and others for humanitarian ❽ _____.

1

Complete the sentences using the words in the list.

> survey   unwind   meditation   assignment   facilities   acupuncture

1. Disabled visitors are welcome; there is good wheelchair access to most _____.
2. _____, which uses needles, can be effective for the relief of pain.
3. He didn't do his school _____ until the very last minute.
4. She found peace through yoga and _____.
5. The _____ indicates that job satisfaction has fallen to its lowest level in 20 years.
6. Listening to music helps me _____ after a busy day.

2

A **Joe is taking the survey. Listen and check (✓) his responses on the survey form.**

CD2 36

Are You Stressed?

Strongly disagree <------------------> Strongly agree

     1 2 3 4 5

1	☐ ☐ ☐ ☐ ☐	I sometimes have trouble sleeping and feel tired during the day.
2	☐ ☐ ☐ ☐ ☐	I find I'm working really hard, but not achieving enough.
3	☐ ☐ ☐ ☐ ☐	I often forget appointments, deadlines, and personal items.
4	☐ ☐ ☐ ☐ ☐	I sometimes get angry with my friends and argue with them.
5	☐ ☐ ☐ ☐ ☐	I don't have much time to relax or do things that I like.
6	☐ ☐ ☐ ☐ ☐	I often get ill with things like colds, headaches, and an upset stomach.
7	☐ ☐ ☐ ☐ ☐	I often have to study or work late into the evening.
8	☐ ☐ ☐ ☐ ☐	I don't have much time to eat, and I often eat fast food.

9	▢▢▢▢	I worry a lot about my weight and looks.
10	▢▢▢▢	I often leave assignments to the last minute and then rush them.
11	▢▢▢▢	I often get annoyed at little things like missing a bus.
12	▢▢▢▢	I think I'm more stressed than most other people.

12–20: You have a pretty stress-free life!
21–40: You need to take care with your stress levels, but overall you are OK.
41–60: You are too stressed.

B Listen again to check your answers. What is Joe's stress level score? 🎧 CD2 36

_____

3

A Joe is asking his friends for advice. Listen and match each piece of advice (a–h) to the correct person. One is extra. 🎧 CD2 37

- **Lisa** _____
- **Ken** _____
- **Geri** _____

a. Take a vacation	**b.** Try self-hypnosis
c. Go for a massage	**d.** Go to a spa
e. Listen to music	**f.** Go to bed early
g. Give up smoking	**h.** Attend a yoga class

B Listen again and fill in the following blanks. 🎧 CD2 37

1. Joe got a really _____ on the survey in Helen's magazine.

2. Following Lisa's advice, Joe will _____
_____.

3. Joe will not follow Ken's advice because he does not want to _____.

4. Joe is interested in Spa Heaven, where he can get _____.

Listen to the conversation. What are three activities the man seems to be interested in? Write the cost of them in the chart below.

Spa Heaven Your Downtown Oasis

Is the pace of modern life stressing you out? Do you find you have no time to unwind and relax? Take a break from the daily grind at Spa Heaven, a newly-opened relaxation complex in a convenient downtown location. Spa Heaven is the perfect place to get away from it all. Come and revitalize yourself at our city oasis!

Our wide range of relaxation facilities includes:

Fitness	Our extensive fitness center offers state-of-the-art strength training equipment. Next to the gym is our aerobics room, where classes are held every morning. Come and experience a total work out!
Sports	Spa Heaven's sporting facilities include two 25-meter swimming pools. Jacuzzi facilities and steam and sauna rooms are also available. Tennis fans will appreciate our six full-size tennis courts, including two indoor courts—so you can play whatever the weather!
Meditation	In this oasis of quiet, you'll be able to find a place of total relaxation. Yoga classes are offered every day, to help you achieve a perfect balance of body, mind, and soul.
Massage	Our individual massage rooms provide total privacy. Feel the everyday effects of modern-day stress disappear at the hands of our experienced masseurs. We offer a wide range of professional massage techniques including reflexology, aromatherapy, and shiatsu.
Acupuncture	If you suffer from aches, tense muscles, or tiredness, try our acupuncture sessions. The traditional techniques of acupuncture are painless and soothing. They will help reduce tension and bring you deep relaxation.

Call 555-7967 for membership details.

	Activity	Cost
1.		$
2.		$
3.		$

1. The man wants to find some way to reduce his stress. **T / F**
2. The special offer has just ended at the end of the month. **T / F**
3. The man is not interested in getting healthy. **T / F**
4. It costs $10 to become a member who can use the pools. **T / F**
5. Acupuncture sessions cost $30 per hour. **T / F**

5 Listen and fill in the survey for Erica.

1. **What kinds of exercise do you do?**
   ☐ Golf ☐ Running ☐ Swimming ☐ Other: _____

2. **What do you do to relax?**
   ☐ Movies ☐ Music ☐ Hanging out ☐ Other: _____

3. **Which of the following do you eat?**
   ☐ Meat ☐ Chicken ☐ Fish ☐ Vegetables

4. **How often do you drink alcohol?**
   ☐ Often ☐ Sometimes ☐ Never

5. **How often do you smoke?**
   ☐ Often ☐ Sometimes ☐ Never

6. **When do you go to bed?**
   ☐ Before 9:00 ☐ 9:00–10:30 ☐ 10:30–12:00 ☐ After 12:00

6 Listen to the descriptions of the two spas. Fill in the information for each one.

CD2
40
▼
41

1. **The Pine Tree Spa**

   Location: _____

   Facilities: _____

   _____

   Tel. No.: _____

2. **The Oasis of Calm**

   Location: _____

   Facilities: _____

   _____

   Tel. No.: _____

Your Turn!

Asking and talking about stress and relaxation

Try this . . .

What causes you stress? Use the survey in Task 2 and interview your partner to find out how stressed he or she is. How does he or she deal with stress?

- What's the most stressful thing for you?

  — I worry about . . .

- So how do you deal with stress?

  — What usually works best for me is to talk over my problems with my family or friends.

- What do you do when you want to unwind?

  — The best way to unwind is to relax at home and just watch TV.

Putting your best foot forward

Listen and fill in the following blanks to complete the passage. ◉ T-13

Massage has long been a popular

❶ _____ of alleviating stress.

A wall painting found in a ❷ _____

at Saqqara, Egypt, clearly shows that foot massage,

also known as reflexology, was practiced more than

❸ _____ years ago. Reflexology is

a natural healing art ❹ _____ on the

principle that there are reflexes in the feet, and also

in the hands and ears, that ❺ _____

to every other part of the body (see picture). It is

believed that by ❻ _____ pressure

to these reflexes, ❼ _____ can be

reduced and body ❽ _____

improved.

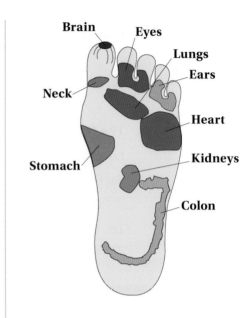

1 Complete the sentences using the words in the list. Be sure to use the correct form of the word.

robbery	involve	standstill	arrest	bystander	injury

1. The policeman _____ him for drunken driving last night.
2. A bomb exploded in a subway station, but amazingly, there were no deaths or _____.
3. Traffic was brought to a _____ by the accident.
4. She is _____ in several volunteer groups.
5. The police arrested several innocent _____ during the riot.
6. There has been a _____ at a branch of the City Bank.

2 Listen to the radio news items and fill in the following blanks.

1. There was a _____ during the first round of judging at the Miss World Contest.

2. _____ houses were destroyed as winds ripped through the city.

3. The robbery was carried out by an _____.

4. Today the stock exchange had the _____ day of the week.

5. The dollar remained _____ against leading world currencies.

Listen for it

Late-breaking is a word used in news reports to indicate a story or fact that has just been reported.

3

Listen to the news reports and answer the following questions.

CD2 47 ▼ 49

1. In which round did he knock out his opponent? _____

2. How old is the suspect? _____

3. How many people are thought to have been washed out to sea? _____

4

A **Listen. What is this announcement? Check (✓) the correct answer.**

CD2 50

☐ Weather report   ☐ News report   ☐ Traffic report   ☐ Sports report

B **Listen again and circle the best answer.**

CD2 50

1. What is this report called?
   a. The Channel 12 TrafficCopter
   b. The Channel Two TrafficCopter

2. What caused this accident?
   a. A car hit a passing truck.
   b. Two trucks hit each other.

3. How is traffic now?
   a. Traffic has completely stopped in one direction.
   b. Traffic has completely stopped in both directions.

C **Listen again and answer the following questions about the key information.**

CD2 50

1. What is being described? _____

2. Where is it? _____

3. What advice does the second speaker give? _____

5

A **Listen to the news report and number the pictures (1–5).**

CD2 51

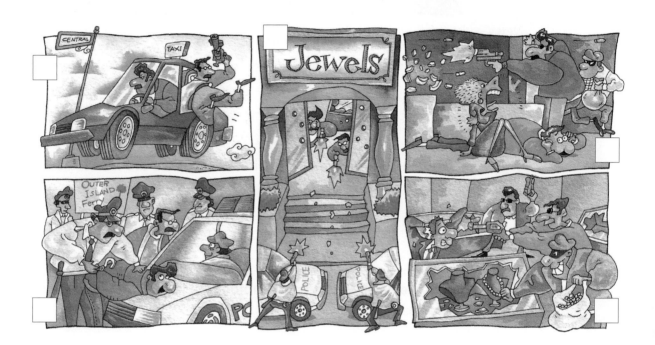

B **Listen again and circle *T* for *True* or *F* for *False*.**

CD2 51

1. The police have arrested four thieves who broke into a jewelry store.   **T / F**

2. The thieves broke into a bank on Center Street.   **T / F**

3. The thieves stole a million dollars in cash.   **T / F**

4. During the gun battle, a bystander was shot in the arm.   **T / F**

5. The injured bystander was taken to the hospital, where she is expected to completely recover.   **T / F**

6. The thieves were caught at the ferry terminal.   **T / F**

6

A Listen to Nick tell his coworker about the robbery. What information does he get wrong? Fill in the chart.

	Where?	What?	How many robbers?	Who was hurt?	What happened?
News account	Center Street	Jewelry store	Three	Female bystander	Caught by police
Nick's account					

B Listen again. Where does Nick think the robbers are now?

7

A Listen to the news reports and number the items (1–5) in the order that you hear them.

- Weather   _____
- Economic news   _____
- Sporting news   _____
- International news   _____
- Local news   _____

B Listen again and circle *T* for *True* or *F* for *False*.

1. The presidents of the United States and Russia met today.   **T / F**
2. The stock market fell.   **T / F**
3. People were injured in an accident.   **T / F**
4. Plans for the Grand Prix racing event have changed.   **T / F**
5. It will be cold tomorrow.   **T / F**
6. Tomorrow is Thursday.   **T / F**

Your Turn!

Asking and talking about news stories

Try this . . .

Ask a partner the questions in the "News Survey." Add a question of your own. Ask follow-up questions to find out more information.

	News Survey	Details
1.	What types of news interest you most?	
2.	What types of news do not interest you?	
3.	What is the biggest news story now?	
4.	What is the best news source?	
5.	_____?	

All the news that's fit to print

Listen and fill in the following blanks to complete the passage. T-14

"The real trends in journalism in the past thirty years have been toward gossip, sensationalism, manufactured controversy, and . . . the dumbing down of most American journalism." —former *Washington Post* reporter Carl Bernstein

For years, ❶ _____ in America and elsewhere have been ❷ _____ about the so-called "tabloidization" of the media: the ❸ _____ toward new and more entertainment-oriented kinds of news, and the placing of a greater ❹ _____ on pictures than on words in both newspapers and TV news broadcasts. ❺ _____ of "tabloidization" argue that it ❻ _____ their ability to keep the public well-informed on important ❼ _____. On the other side are those who say the modern ❽ _____ is only giving the people what they want.

14 Talking about people you admire

1 **Complete the sentences using the words in the list.**

dignified	exhibition	inspiration
creativity	influence	admire

1. _____ and originality are more important than technical skills.

2. Many people worry about the _____ violent movies have on children.

3. Genius is one percent _____ and 99 percent perspiration.

4. I _____ those who work hard to make a living.

5. He was _____ and calm during the ceremony.

6. The painting was damaged during its _____.

2 **Listen to the three conversations. Complete the following scripts.**   CD2 54 ~ 56

1. **M1:** You know, I met him _____. It was at a party at the embassy.

   M2: Yeah? What was he like?

   M1: Oh, he was really _____. He was so _____.

   M2: Yeah, he looks like that on TV. I think he's so _____.

2. **W:** Don't you think she's a _____ singer?

   M: Well, I don't like her style much, but I guess I'd have to say yes.

3. **W:** So, what do you think of her?

   M: Oh, I think she's so _____.

   W: So do I. She was great during the Oscars.

A Listen. Check (✓) the words used to describe each person.

1.

Alan

☐ sensitive
☐ generous
☐ serious
☐ intelligent

2.

Jenny

☐ caring
☐ wise
☐ calm
☐ angry

3.

Tracy

☐ angry
☐ friendly
☐ ambitious
☐ humorous

4.

Greg

☐ energetic
☐ creative
☐ original
☐ talented

B Listen again. What do the speakers admire most about each person? Circle one word for each.

Listen and circle the correct response.

1. **a.** I think she's very talented.
    b. I'm afraid not.
    c. I think she's smart.

2. **a.** He is, isn't he?
    b. He's really smart.
    c. He's still thinking.

3. **a.** No, she's not here.
    b. Not recently.
    c. Yes, fascinating.

4. **a.** He likes playing golf.
    b. I don't like him much.
    c. He's an interesting character.

5. **a.** Thanks, that's kind of you to say so.
    b. I can't describe it.
    c. I'm not sure.

6. **a.** I love sleeping.
    b. I don't know. I just am.
    c. I guess it's interesting.

5

A **Listen to the conversation and circle the best answer.**

CD2
62

1. This is . . .
   a. a face-to-face interview.
   b. a survey.
   c. a phone interview.

2. The woman is . . .
   a. an artist.
   b. a reporter.
   c. a photographer.

3. The man is described as . . .
   a. a talented and original person.
   b. an ambitious and creative person.
   c. a talented and creative person.

4. The man's main inspiration comes from . . .
   a. nature.
   b. other exhibitions.
   c. his family.

B **Listen again and circle *T* for *True* or *F* for *False*.**

CD2
62

1. This is the second exhibition.   T / F
2. The first exhibition was held two years ago.   T / F
3. The artist's works are very realistic.   T / F
4. The artist was influenced by Jackson Pollock.   T / F

C **What does the man say about the artist Jackson Pollock?**

_____

6

A **Listen and circle *T* for *True* or *F* for *False*.**

CD2
63

Listen for it

If someone *stands out*, it means he or she is special or different in some way.

1. The interviewee is a soccer fan from Singapore.   T / F
2. He is a supporter of England.   T / F
3. He has met David Beckham.   T / F
4. He thinks Ronaldo is the best Brazilian player ever.   T / F
5. He attended the 2002 World Cup.   T / F

B Listen again. According to the interviewee, what are three qualities that Ronaldo and Beckham have in common?

1. Both are _____ .
2. Both are _____ .
3. Both are _____ .

7

A Listen and circle the best answer.

1. This is . . .
   a. an interview.   **b.** a telephone conversation.   **c.** a casual conversation.

2. The speakers are . . .
   a. brother and sister.   **b.** husband and wife.   **c.** cousins.

3. They are talking about . . .
   a. famous family members.   **b.** people in a magazine.   **c.** personality traits.

B Listen again and fill in the survey for Sharon. Write each person's name and his or her relationship to Sharon.

	Who is . . .	Name	Relationship
1.	the funniest person you know?		
2.	the most energetic person you know?		
3.	the most creative person you know?		
4.	the most interesting person you know?		

Mr. McNeil   **Sally**   **Debbie**   **Simon**

Your Turn!

Talking about people you admire

Try this . . .

Complete the survey with the names of people you know. Tell your partner. Ask about the people your partner has listed. Find out why your partner chose each person.

- Do you know anyone who's really creative?
- Who has the best sense of humor?
- How about the most energetic person?
- Do you know anyone who's really intelligent?
- Who's the most ambitious person you know?

● **Who is the most . . . person you know?**

	You	Your partner / details
creative		
humorous		
energetic		
intelligent		
ambitious		

The importance of being honest

Listen and fill in the following blanks to complete the passage.

T-15

In a recent survey _(1)_____ by *USA Weekend* magazine, U.S. teenagers were asked about the things they most admire in other people of their own age. The most highly admired quality was revealed to be honesty, followed by sense of _(2)_____, intelligence, _(3)_____, and kindness. Students also said they admired people who are good at sports, physically _(4)_____, popular, and rich. When asked who was the biggest influence in their _(5)_____, the majority of respondents said that their parents were the most important influence, _(6)_____ by girlfriend/boyfriend and teacher. _(7)_____ percent of respondents stated that _(8)_____ were a major influence.

15 Asking and talking about medical conditions

1 Complete the sentences using the words in the list.

| appointment | appendix | tonsillitis | surgery | temperature | vomit |

1. _____ means an infection of the tonsils in which they become swollen and sore.
2. The bus ride made her feel so sick that she began to _____.
3. The _____ soared to 30°C this afternoon.
4. She confirmed her _____ with the dentist.
5. He had to have a _____ on his knee.
6. She might have to have her _____ taken out.

2 Alan is talking to a receptionist at a doctor's office. Listen and complete the form.

Medical Report

Official Report

Health Insurance No.: [   ]

Name: _Alan Whitaker_____   Date of Birth: _____

Address: _____

City: _Oakside_____   Phone: _____

Reason for Visit: _____

Medical History: _____

Taking Medication: ☐ Yes _____
                   ☐ No

Allergies: ☐ Yes _____
                   ☐ No

3

A Three people are telling their doctors about different medical problems. Listen and write down the problems.

Listen for it

Ouch! is sometimes used to express sudden pain or displeasure.

	Patient	Problem	Information
1.	Jennifer		
2.	Sarah		
3.	Mandy		

B Listen again. Write down any other information you hear about each patient's problem.

4

A Listen to the doctors and people from Task 3. Write down the doctor's diagnosis for each patient.

	Patient	Diagnosis	Treatment
1.	Jennifer		
2.	Sarah		
3.	Mandy		

B Listen again. What treatment does each doctor prescribe? Choose the correct treatment in the list for each patient and write it in the chart.

cast   operation   medication

5

A Listen to the radio broadcast. Number the topics in the order the doctor talks about them (1–4).

- Exercise _____
- Diet _____
- Smoking _____
- Sleep _____

Listen for it

Overdo means to do too much of something, such as dieting or exercising.

B Listen again and write down Dr. Bain's tips on maintaining good health.

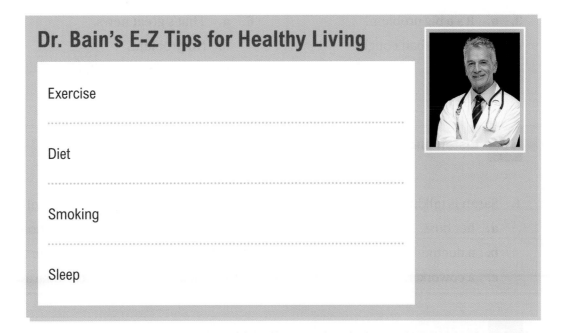

Dr. Bain's E-Z Tips for Healthy Living

Exercise
....

Diet
....

Smoking
....

Sleep

C Listen again and circle *T* for *True* or *F* for *False*.

1. To eat a nutritious diet, you have to give up the foods you love. T / F
2. Artificially produced vitamins cannot be a substitute for the nutrition we derive from food. T / F
3. You need at least eight hours of sleep a night. T / F
4. To maintain good fitness, thirty minutes' exercise is enough. T / F
5. You must not overdo vitamins or alcohol. T / F

6 Listen and circle the correct response.

1. a. I've been coughing.
   b. For about a week.
   c. Why, do you have a cold?

2. a. Yes, the pain is terrible.
   b. No, it's way over there.
   c. Do you think so?

3. a. It's a big problem.
   b. I have a bad cough.
   c. Yes, it is.

4. a. No, my hand.
   b. Yes, I can't stop sneezing.
   c. Yes, my foot hurts.

5. a. I think so.
   b. Yes, twice a day.
   c. No, we don't sell any.

6. a. That's great news.
   b. No problem.
   c. I'm sorry to hear that.

7 **A** Listen and circle the best answer.

1. Sarah is talking to . . .
   a. her boss.
   b. a doctor.
   c. a coworker.

2. They are . . .
   a. at the clinic.
   b. at home.
   c. at the office.

3. Sarah will probably . . .
   a. go home and rest.
   b. go to the hospital.
   c. take a vacation.

B Listen again and check (✓) Sarah's symptoms.

☐ Fever ☐ Sore throat ☐ Vomiting ☐ Rash
☐ Headache ☐ Sneezing ☐ Dizziness

Your Turn!

Asking and talking about medical conditions

Try this . . .

Imagine you are not feeling well. Describe your symptoms to a partner. Answer any questions about your illness. Your partner will make a diagnosis and prescribe treatment.

- What seems to be the problem?
- How long has this been going on?
- Have you got any other symptoms?
- It sounds like you have _____.
- Take this medicine and get a lot of rest.

Medical Consultation Form	
Symptoms:	
Diagnosis:	
Treatment:	
	Official Report

You're making me sick!

Listen and fill in the following blanks to complete the passage.

T-16

Have you ever received news that made you "feel like a million bucks?" Or felt physically ill upon ending a friendship or romantic relationship? If so, your experiences illustrate the

(1) _____ emotions can have on a person's (2) _____ health. Medical (3) _____ have long noted the (4) _____ between physical and emotional health but many people remain (5) _____ that their feelings can actually make them sick. Some doctors argue that (6) _____ emotions can help lead to the development of stomach ulcers and bladder infections among other ailments. On the other hand, there are also cases in which people given to excessive shows of emotion fall (7) _____ to diseases of the heart or

(8) _____ system.

クラス用音声CD有り（非売品）

教師用音声CD有り（非売品）

Hear Me Out 2
実践リスニング徹底演習シリーズ＜中級編＞

2017年1月20日　初版発行
2023年8月20日　Text Only版第1刷

著　者　David Nunan
編著者　富岡紀子
発行者　松村達生
発行所　センゲージ ラーニング株式会社
　　　　〒102-0073　東京都千代田区九段北1-11-11　第2フナトビル5階
　　　　電話 03-3511-4392　FAX 03-3511-4391
　　　　e-mail: eltjapan@cengage.com
　　　　copyright©2017 センゲージ ラーニング株式会社

装　丁　　足立友幸（parastyle）
編集協力　飯尾緑子（parastyle）
印刷・製本　株式会社平河工業社

ISBN 978-4-86312-321-2